AN ILLUSTRATED DATA GUIDE TO

MODERN FAST ATTACK CRAFT

Compiled by
Christopher Chant

**TIGER BOOKS INTERNATIONAL
LONDON**

This edition published in 1997 by
Tiger Books International PLC
Twickenham

Published in Canada in 1997 by
Vanwell Publishing Limited
St. Catharines, Ontario

© Graham Beehag Books
Christchurch
Dorset

Printed in Hong Kong

ISBN 1-85501-862-4

CONTENTS

"Hauk" class
(Norway)

Type: Fast attack craft (missile and torpedo)

Displacement: 120 tons standard and 148 tons full load

Dimensions: Length 119ft 9in (36.5m); beam 20ft 0in (6.1m); draught 5ft 0in (1.5m)

Gun armament: One 40mm Bofors L/70 anti-aircraft gun in a Bofors single mounting, and one 20mm Rheinmetall L/92 anti-aircraft gun in an S20 single mounting

Missile armament: Six single container-launchers for Kongsberg Penguin Mk II (possibly to be supplanted by Penguin Mk III) anti-ship missiles

Torpedo armament: Two single 21in (533mm)

mountings for two FFV Tp 61 wire-guided anti-ship torpedoes

Anti-submarine armament: None

Electronics: Two Racal Decca TM1226 surface-search and navigation radars, one Kongsberg MSI-80S fire-control system (with one TVT-300 optronic tracker and one laser rangefinder), and one Simrad SQ-3D/QF active search hull sonar

Propulsion: Diesel arrangement with two MTU 16V 538 TB92 diesel engines delivering a total of 7,240hp (5,400kW) to two shafts

Performance: Maximum speed 34kt; range 505 miles (815km) at 34kt

Complement: 20

Precursors to the 14 craft of the "Hauk" class, the six units of the "Snögg" class (here represented by the Rapp) were the steel-hulled counterparts to the wooden-hulled "Storm" class.

Norway (Hauk class)

Name	No.	Builder	Commissioned
Hauk	P986	Bergens Mek	Aug 1977
Ørn	P987	Bergens Mek	Jan 1979
Terne	P988	Bergens Mek	Mar 1979
Tjeld	P989	Bergens Mek	May 1979
Skarv	P990	Bergens Mek	Jul 1979
Teist	P991	Bergens Mek	Sep 1979
Jo	P992	Bergens Mek	Nov 1979
Lom	P993	Bergens Mek	Jan 1980
Stegg	P994	Bergens Mek	Mar 1980
Falk	P995	Bergens Mek	Apr 1980
Ravn	P996	Westamarin	May 1980
Gribb	P997	Westamarin	Jul 1980
Geir	P998	Westamarin	Sep 1980
Erle	P999	Westamarin	Dec 1980

Notes

Of the four members of the Scandinavian community, the country whose navy makes the greatest use of the FAC in its operational planning and procurement is Norway, its comparatively short southern coastline dominating the Skagerrak, the western half of the exit from the Baltic Sea into the North Sea. Far longer, however, are Norway's western and northern coastlines, which stretch from the North Sea through the Norwegian Sea and into the Arctic Ocean. Open-sea conditions in these areas can be rough in the extreme, and indeed far too dangerous for sustained operations by fast combat craft, and the Norwegian navy is faced with the difficult tactical problem of defending one of the longest coastlines in the world with only modest funding, as the country has only a small population. A significant submarine force is maintained, together with a small number of obsolescent deep-water warships, but the main strength of the Norwegian navy rests with its force of fast combat craft. These are ideally suited to coastal operations along Norway's littoral, which is scattered with the islands and fjords that make excellent lurking and hunting grounds for torpedo- and missile-armed FACs.

At the end of World War II, the Norwegian navy was re-established in its own country with ex-British destroyers and escorts, ex-German submarines, and light forces that comprised ex-British motor torpedo boats (MTBs) and ex-

German *Schnellboote* (E-boats). Between 1951 and 1956 the Norwegian builder Båtservice delivered from its Mandal yard six MTBs of the "Rapp" class as Norway's first indigenously produced fast combat craft. The craft proved well suited to operational conditions in Norwegian waters, but had Packard engines using dangerously inflammable petrol as fuel.

This was a primary reason for the development of the "Nasty" class, which was built to the extent of 42 craft between 1959 and 1967, to a fairly standard MTB design with a full-load displacement of 77 tons on a hull that measured 80ft 5in (24.5m) in length and 24ft 7in (7.5m) in beam. This hull was of unusual construction for the period, however, for it was a sandwich of fibreglass between two layers of mahogany. The petrol-engined propulsion arrangement of the "Rapp" class was abandoned in favour of a diesel-engined arrangement with two lightweight Napier Deltic T 18-37 diesel engines delivering 6,200hp (4,620kW) to two shafts for a maximum speed of 43kt. The boats were completed with provision for two basic armament fits to create MTBs or motor gun boats (MGBs). The MTB fit was centred on four 21in (533mm) tubes for heavyweight anti-ship torpedoes, and included one 40mm Bofors gun and one 20mm cannon, while the MGB sacrificed two of the tubes so that the 20mm cannon could be replaced by a second 40mm Bofors gun. The boats could also be used as minelayers by unshipping all the tubes. The Norwegian navy received 20 such boats as the "Tjeld" class, and these have now faded from service. The other 22 boats were exported.

Like the Soviets and other major operators of FACs in the early 1960s, Norway decided that the best tactical effect could be gained from the use of mixed FAC(T) and FAC(M) forces. The anti-ship missile was still in its infancy as a weapon type, and Norway decided to produce its own weapon to ensure that it would be fully optimised for the operational requirements imposed by Norway's geographic situation. The result was the West's first dedicated anti-ship missile, the Kongsberg Penguin based on an infra-red seeker (the first completely passive seeker fitted on any surface-to-surface missile) and the warhead of the ASM-N-7/AGM-12 Bullpup, an air-to-surface missile of American design. The missile is delivered as a maintenance-free round in a container that is installed on the deck of the FAC to serve as a launcher after the necessary umbilical electrical connection has been made.

The Norwegian navy decided that, as the missions planned for craft with this missile would be of short range and minimal endurance, habitability could be partially sacrificed to a larger number of missiles on the type of small hull that was best suited to operations in Norwegian coastal waters. The result was the "Storm" class of FAC(M)s, comprising 20 craft commissioned between 1965 and 1968. This type has a full-load displacement of only 135 tons on a hull that has a maximum length of 119ft 9in (36.5m) and beam of 20ft 0in (6.1m). Power as well as habitability had to be sacrificed, however, and each of the "Storm" class craft has only two 3,620hp (2,700kW) Maybach MD 872A (later redesignated MTU 16V 538) diesel engines for a maximum speed of just 32kt, which is perhaps adequate for the type of "hide and seek" operations planned by the Norwegians. The armament is impressive, for in addition to six Penguin Mk I anti-ship missiles (introduced in 1972 and now supplemented by the longer-range Penguin Mk II with an improved seeker), each of these craft carries two Bofors guns in the form of one forecastle-mounted 76mm (3in) automatic weapon for the surface-to-surface role and one stern-mounted 40mm calibre weapon for the anti-aircraft role. The electronic fit was adequate, but was upgraded in the late 1980s and early 1990s with a modern fire-control system that includes an optronic tracker and a laser rangefinder.

In 1970 and 1971, Norway supplemented the "Storm" class craft with the six "Snögg" class craft, which are based on a hull that is essentially a steel version of the wooden hull used in the "Storm" class. The performance of the "Snögg" class is roughly comparable with that of the "Storm" class for obvious operational reasons, but the weapon fit was modified to turn these craft into FAC(M/T)s. Thus the 76mm (3in) gun was removed and its place taken by the 40mm weapon in an open mounting, leaving the after part of the deck clear for a quartet of container-launchers for Penguin missiles. The armament is completed by four deck-edge 21in (533mm) tubes for Swedish wire-guided heavyweight anti-ship torpedoes. Like the "Storm" class, the "Snögg" class initially possessed only moderately advanced electronics, but in recent years these have been upgraded with an improved torpedo fire-control system as well as the same surface-weapon fire-control system as the updated "Storm" class craft. Even so, it must be conceded that both classes are now obsolescent.

The Hauk is lead craft of a 14-strong class developed as successor to the six-strong "Snögg" class, and is seen here with its forward-mounted armament of one 40mm Bofors gun and two 21in (533mm) torpedo tubes.

By the mid-1970s the Norwegian navy had appreciated this slide into obsolescence and had begun the process of developing a successor type on the basis of the *Jägaren*, which was the Norwegian-built prototype for the Swedish "Hugin" class. This resulted in the 14 units of the "Hauk" class that were commissioned between 1977 and 1980, and represented an updated development of the "Snögg" class with a more capable fire-control system. This type has a full-load displacement of 148 tons and the standard Norwegian propulsion arrangement of two diesel engines delivering a total of 7,240hp (5,400kW) to two shafts for a maximum speed of 34kt. The gun armament comprises the typical 40mm Bofors weapon as well as a 20mm cannon, the missile fit is six container-launchers for Penguin missiles, and additional capability is provided by two 21in (533mm) tubes for Swedish wire-guided heavyweight torpedoes. The electronics are of the upgraded standard retrofitted in the "Storm" and "Snögg" classes, but an unusual feature is the provision for active search sonar even though the craft carry no dedicated anti-submarine armament. During the 1990s the craft were modernised for better air-defence capability with the SIMBAD twin launcher for Matra Mistral short-range surface-to-air missiles with infra-red homing.

"Helsinki" class
(Finland)

Type: Fast attack craft (missile and gun)

Displacement: 280 tons standard and 300 tons full load

Dimensions: Length 147ft 8in (45.0m); beam 29ft 2in (8.9m); draught 9ft 10in (3.0m)

Gun armament: One 57mm Bofors SAK 57 Mk 2 L/70 dual-purpose gun in a Bofors single mounting, and four 23mm L/60 anti-aircraft guns in two twin mountings

Missile armament: Four single container-launchers for four Saab RBS 15M anti-ship missiles

Torpedo armament: None

Anti-submarine armament: Two depth-charge rails

Electronics: One Bofors Electronics 9GA 208 surface-search radar, one tracking radar used in conjunction with one Bofors Electronics 9LV 225 fire-control system, one Saab EOS 40 optronic director, one Simrad SS 304 active search hull sonar, and one ESM system with a Marconi Matilda radar-warning element

Propulsion: Diesel arrangement with three MTU 16V 538 TB92 diesel engines delivering 10,965hp (8,175kW) to three shafts

Performance: Maximum speed 30kt

Complement: 30

Seen here on trials with the 57mm Bofors SAK57 Mk 2 dual-purpose gun as its sole armament, the Helsinki is lead craft of the Finnish navy's four-strong "Helsinki" class. The class is notable for its nicely balanced multi-role armament and moderately high level of electronic sophistication.

Finland (Helsinki class)			
Name	No.	Builder	Commissioned
Helsinki	60	Wärtsilä	Sep 1981
Turku	61	Wärtsilä	Jun 1985
Oulu	62	Wärtsilä	Oct 1985
Kotka	63	Wärtsilä	Jun 1986

Notes

In addition to financial considerations, it was the particular geographical and tactical conditions of the Baltic Sea that persuaded three of the four Scandinavian nations (Finland, Sweden and Denmark) to make FACs a major component of their naval defences against possible Soviet aggression from the early 1950s. Like Sweden, Finland is a neutral state, although in this instance as a result not only of natural inclination but also of international mandate in the form of the February 1947 Treaty of Paris. This was a consequence of Finland's role as a German ally in World War II, and among the Treaty's provisions was a navy of not more than 10,000 tons and 4,500 men. Submarines and torpedoes were specifically forbidden to the Finnish navy at the demand of the Soviets, who feared that such weapons could effectively deny them use of Leningrad (now St Petersburg) as a base, as this major city and its naval base lie at the head of the Gulf of Finland. Finland thus had to delete its five submarines and remove the torpedo tubes from its MTBs. Since that time, the Finnish navy has received relatively little in the way of funding, and has concentrated its efforts on

two conventional corvettes and larger forces of mine warfare vessels, patrol vessels and fast combat craft.

The patrol vessels form a flotilla based at Helsinki, and comprise the three and two units respectively of the "Ruissalo" and "Rihtniemi" classes of large patrol craft. Armed with a 40mm Bofors gun and capable of only 15kt, these craft are of little real operational value. Launched between 1956 and 1959, these five craft were joined in the 1960s by 13 units of the "Nuoli" class of gun-armed FACs. Although fast as a result of their powerplant of three Soviet M 50 diesel engines delivering a total of 3,620hp (2,700kW) to three shafts for a speed of 40kt, these craft were armed only with a 40mm Bofors gun and therefore were of limited combat value. By the late 1960s, the Finnish navy had become fully aware of the importance of the anti-ship missile, and in December 1969 launched the *Isku* as an experimental FAC(M). With a full-load displacement of 140 tons, this singleton unit was based on the hull of a landing craft (and thus capable of only 18kt) and was commissioned in 1970 as a trials and training type. The armament comprises two 30mm cannon in a twin mounting above the after part of the superstructure, and four container-launchers for the MTO/68 anti-ship missile (the Finnish designation for the Soviet SS-N-2A "Styx').

Experience with the *Isku* made it sensible for the Finns to order four Soviet "Osa" class craft in the early 1970s, and these were delivered in 1974 and 1975 for completion with Finnish electronics and Western radar under the designation "Tuima" class. By 1980, the Finns had sufficient experience with these four craft to consider a locally designed type, and this matured as the aluminium-hulled "Helsinki" class designed for a 30-year operational life. The design was proved in the *Helsinki* that was commissioned in 1981 as a true FAC(M/G) with a combination of Swedish and Soviet guns as well as a powerful combination of Swedish anti-ship missiles and Swedish radar. The Finns then ordered another three "Helsinki" class units to a revised standard that was later applied to the *Helsinki*.

The limited and now obsolescent short-range defensive capability provided by the paired 23mm Soviet cannon is to be improved by the adoption of a genuine close-in weapon system mounting.

"Helsinki 2" or "Rauma" class
(Finland)

Type: Fast attack craft (missile and gun)

Displacement: 215 tons standard and 248 tons full load

Dimensions: Length 157ft 6in (48.0m); beam 26ft 3in (8.0m); draught 5ft 0in (1.5m)

Gun armament: One 40mm Bofors L/70 anti-aircraft gun in a Bofors single mounting, and provision (if the SADRAL launcher is not shipped) for two 23mm anti-aircraft guns in a twin mounting

Missile armament: Typically, six or maximum eight single container-launchers for six or eight Saab RBS 15M anti-ship missiles, and one SADRAL sextuple launcher for six Matra Mistral short-range surface-to-air missiles

Torpedo armament: None

Anti-submarine armament: One Saab Elma grenade system with four LLS-920 nine-barrel launchers, and one depth-charge rail

Electronics: One Bofors Electronics 9GA 208 surface-search radar, one Raytheon ARPA navigation radar, one tracking radar used in conjunction with one Bofors Electronics 9LV 225 fire-control system, one Bofors Electronics 9LV 200 Mk 3 Sea Viking optronic director (with TV, FLIR and laser sensors), one Simrad Toadfish search and attack hull sonar, and one Bofors Electronics 9LW 300 ESM system with one Marconi Matilda radar-warning element and an unrevealed number of Bofors Electronics Philax decoy and chaff/flare launchers

Propulsion: Diesel arrangement with two MTU 16V 538 TB92 diesel engines delivering a total of 7,510hp (5,600kW) to two Riva Calzoni waterjets

Performance: Maximum speed 30kt

Complement: 5+14

Finland			
Name	No.	Builder	Commissioned
Rauma	70	Hollming	May 1990
	71	Hollming	1991
	72	Hollming	1992
	73	Hollming	1992

Notes

These first four craft were ordered in August 1987 at the start of the "Helsinki 2" (later "Rauma') class programme that envisaged a total of 12 such craft, although the end of the "Cold War" and the subsequent decline of tension in Europe has unsettled the plans for the final eight units.

The craft were built with only six anti-ship missiles, although there is deck space and electronic capacity for eight missiles to be shipped. It had originally been planned that the craft would be completed with a more capable dual-purpose gun, the 57mm Bofors SAK 57 Mk 2 L/70 weapon, but it was then decided to retain the smaller and older 40mm Bofors L/70 weapon in combination with a capable short-range surface-to-air missile system of French origin, which itself can be replaced by a pair of 23mm Soviet cannon in a twin mounting.

Notable features of the design are a higher level of automation to allow the use of a smaller crew, a length/beam ratio considerably higher than that of the preceding "Helsinki" class, lighter standard and full-load displacements despite the carriage of a heavy missile armament used in conjunction with a more advanced electronic fit, and the use of two rather than three diesel engines in combination with waterjet propulsion for greater economy without sacrificing performance. Like the four units of the "Helsinki" class, the four craft of the "Rauma" class can also be configured for the mine warfare role, which is very important in the shallow waters of the Baltic.

"Hugin" class
(Sweden)

Type: Fast attack craft (missile and gun)

Displacement: 120 tons standard and 150 tons full load

Dimensions: Length 120ft 0in (36.6m); beam 20ft 8in (6.3m); draught 5ft 7in (1.7m)

Gun armament: One 57mm Bofors SAK 57 Mk1 L/70 dual-purpose gun in a Bofors single mounting

Missile armament: Six single container-launchers for six Kongsberg RB 12 (Penguin Mk II) anti-ship missiles (to be replaced by Saab RBS 15M anti-ship missiles)

Torpedo armament: None

Anti-submarine armament: One Saab Elma grenade system with four LLS-920 nine-barrel launchers, and two depth-charge racks

Mines: 24 on two rails (optional replacement for missiles)

Electronics: One Skanter Mk 009 surface-search and navigation radar, one tracking radar used in conjunction with one Bofors Electronics 9LV 200 Mk 2 fire-control system, one Simrad SQ-3D/SF active search and attack hull sonar, and one ESM system with one Saab EWS 905 warning element and two Bofors Electronics Philax chaff/flare decoy launchers

Propulsion: Diesel arrangement with two MTU 20V 672 TY90 diesel engines delivering a total of 7,200hp (5,370kW) to two shafts

Performance: Maximum speed 36kt; range 620 miles (1,000km) at 35kt

Complement: 3+19

Sweden (Hugin class)

Name	No.	Builder	Commissioned
Hugin	P151	Bergens Mek	Jul 1978
Munin	P152	Bergens Mek	Jul 1978
Magne	P153	Bergens Mek	Oct 1978
Mode	P154	Westamarin	Jan 1979
Vale	P155	Westamarin	Apr 1979
Vidar	P156	Westamarin	Aug 1979
Mjölner	P157	Westamarin	Oct 1979
Mysing	P158	Westamarin	Feb 1980
Kaparen	P159	Bergens Mek	Aug 1980
Väktaren	P160	Bergens Mek	Sep 1980
Snapphanen	P161	Bergens Mek	Jan 1980
Spejaren	P162	Bergens Mek	Mar 1980
Styrbjörn	P163	Bergens Mek	Jun 1980
Starkodder	P164	Bergens Mek	Aug 1981
Tordön	P165	Bergens Mek	Oct 1981
Tirfing	P166	Bergens Mek	Jan 1982

Notes

Sweden, a political neutral which wished to preserve its traditional neutrality in the period between the end of World War II and the start of the "Cold War", decided to strengthen its policy of maintaining armed forces that could deter aggression or, failing this, defeat an invasion that could realistically come only from across the Baltic Sea. Its navy was therefore the first line of defence, initially with a conventional but obsolescent or obsolete force of coast-defence battleships, cruisers and destroyers as the core of three task forces. It soon became clear that these forces were of little military value, and that far better value for money could be obtained from lighter forces that would also be more effective. Thus, from 1958, the concept of the "light navy" emerged, of perhaps two major surface warships, small but powerfully armed submarines, two flotillas of torpedo-armed fast combat craft, and a larger number of coast-defence flotillas equipped with MTBs.

In the early 1950s, Sweden built 10 'T 32' class MTBs with a standard displacement of 38.5 tons, an armament of one 40mm Bofors gun and two 21in (533mm) torpedoes, and a maximum speed of 45kt on the power of three 1,500hp (1,118kW) Isotta-Fraschini 184C petrol engines. These craft were deleted in the early 1970s, but had already been supplemented and effectively supplanted by the 15 slightly larger MTBs of the 'T 42' class built between 1955 and 1957 with a 4- ton standard displacement but basically the same armament and performance as the preceding boats. By the late 1940s, however, the Swedish navy had already come to appreciate that such boats were useful only for inshore defence. For true coastal defence, a larger type was necessary and here the Swedish navy turned to the acknowledged leader in this field, Lürrsen of Vegesack, the World War II designer of Germany's *Schnellboote* E-boats. A prototype was built in 1950 as the *Perseus* with a CODAG (COmbined Diesel And Gas turbine) propulsion arrangement of one gas turbine and two diesel engines, and this paved the way for the "Plejad" class of diesel-powered FAC(T)s that eventually totalled 12 craft (including the prototype) built in two batches as six craft between 1954 and 1955, and another five craft between 1956 and 1958. Of the 11 definitive craft, eight were deleted in July 1977 and the last three in July 1981.

This type may be regarded as the Western starting point for the design of modern FACs. The hull had an overall length of 157ft 6in (48.0m) and a beam of 19ft 0in (5.8m) for a full-load displacement of 170 tons. The propulsion arrangement comprised three 3,020hp (2,250kW) MTU 20V 672 diesel engines powering three propellers for a maximum speed of 37.5kt. The bridge structure was located just forward of the amidships point, and the armament comprised two guns and six 21in (533mm) tubes for heavyweight torpedoes. The barrelled weapons were remotely controlled 40mm Bofors guns in mountings on the forecastle and on the after deck midway between the bridge and the stern, and the torpedo tubes were located as three on each side of the deck to fire wire-guided torpedoes: of these tubes, the forward pair were located outboard of the forward 40mm gun mounting and aligned almost directly ahead, while the two after pairs were located as side-by-side installations outboard of the after 40mm gun mounting and designed to fire more obliquely outboard so that the torpedoes would clear the turbulent water of the wake streaming back from the bow. The torpedoes were exceptional weapons by the standards of the day, offering considerable speed and range as well as excellent targeting accuracy with a large high-explosive warhead. Extra operational flexibility was provided by the fact that the torpedo tubes could be unshipped, allowing the craft to operate as minelayers.

Operational experience convinced the Swedes that in such a FAC(T) they had a highly capable type that was fast and effective in virtually all coastal conditions. The torpedoes provided considerable offensive striking power, and the Bofors guns offered a powerful primary anti-aircraft defence as well as a secondary surface-to-surface capability against smaller vessels such as enemy FACs and landing craft.

In the circumstances, it was inevitable that the Swedish navy should capitalise on the advantages provided by this pioneering FAC and develop a series of improved types. The first step was the commissioning, between 1966 and 1968, of the six "Spica" (later "Spica I") class FAC(T)s. The design of these craft was not merely an upgraded version of the "Plejad" class design, but rather a considerable reworking of the original FAC(T) concept to take full advantage of technical developments of the late 1950s and early 1960s in fields such as propulsion, weapons and sensors. The "Spica I" class therefore switched to gas turbine propulsion, using three 4,240hp (3,160kW) Bristol (later Rolls-Royce) Proteus 1274 gas turbines powering three shafts for a maximum speed of 40kt. The more compact nature of the gas turbine powerplant allowed a slight reduction in overall length of 140ft 1in (42.5m) but an increase in beam to 23ft 4in (7.1m) for a full-load displacement of 235 tons. Sensor developments allowed the incorporation of Skanter Mk 009 surface-search and navigation radar and also the Hollandse Signaalapparaten WM-22 fire-control system with co-mounted search and tracking radar antennae in the single spherical glassfibre radome carried above the bridge. This was located farther aft than in the "Plejad" class craft to allow the installation on the forecastle of a significantly improved gun, the 57mm Bofors SAK 57 automatic weapon. Its siting gave this weapon excellent fields of fire, and the Swedes reckoned that in combination with

an advanced fire-control system, its calibre, accuracy, lethal projectile, high rates of traverse and elevation, and high rate of fire (200 rounds per minute) made it a more effective anti-aircraft weapon than current surface-to-air missile systems; the gun also possessed a most useful surface-to-surface capability, which enhanced its overall tactical utility.

The torpedo armament was basically similar to that of the "Plejad" class, with two tubes flanking the gun (in a location where they have to be swung out through several degrees before torpedoes can be launched) and the other four in side-by-side pairs flanking the rear part of the superstructure, and could be unshipped to allow the craft to serve as minelayers. The Swedes prepared plans for two or all four of the after torpedo tubes to be replaced by four or eight container-launchers for anti-ship missiles, but this plan was never implemented and all 12 "Spica I" class craft were deleted in the later 1980s.

Further evolution of the same basic design concept resulted in the 12 units of the "Spica II" class (see separate entry). To increase the overall capabilities of their FAC forces, the Swedes then decided to add a fairly substantial FAC(M) type to its FAC forces, this smaller but missile-armed class complementing the larger craft with a mixed torpedo and missile armament. The result was the "Hugin" class, whose 16 units were commissioned between 1978 and 1982. The design was evaluated in a prototype, the *Jägaren*, which was completed in 1972 as a Swedish derivative of the Norwegian "Snögg" class design. The *Jägaren* underwent considerable evaluation and development before the "Hugin" class was ordered from two Norwegian yards in May 1975; Sweden supplied the guns and electronics together with the machinery, which comprised the engines removed from the "Plejad" class craft and returned to West Germany for overhaul and uprating by MTU before redelivery to Norway.

In an effort to keep cost to a minimum, the design was completed with a two- rather than three-engined propulsion arrangement, and this results in a maximum speed of 35kt on a full-load displacement of 150 tons. The electronic suite includes search radar and the Mk 2 digital version of the 9LV 200 Mk I analogue fire-control system used in the "Spica II" class craft, while the weapons include the 57mm SAK 57 Mk I dual-purpose gun on the forecastle forward of the bridge, and six container-launchers for the RB 12 anti-ship missile. The latter weapon is a Swedish/Norwegian development of an important Norwegian weapon, the Kongsberg Penguin Mk II, which uses an inertial navigation system for the cruise phase of its flight and a passive infra-red seeker package for the terminal phase of the attack.

The class is still in valuable service for use in the Swedish archipelago and the Baltic, and some of the craft have been retrofitted with variable-depth sonar, reflecting Sweden's fears in the late 1980s about Soviet (now Russian) coastal submarine capability. The class is also being cycled through a mid-life modernisation programme to include a new hull-mounted sonar, improved anti-submarine weapons, improved automation of the action data system, and low-speed machinery.

"La Combattante II" class
(France/Greece)

Type: Fast attack craft (missile and torpedo)

Displacement: 324 tons standard and 255 tons full load

Dimensions: Length 154ft 3in (47.0m); beam 23ft 3in (7.1m); draught 8ft 3in (2.5m)

Gun armament: Four 35mm Oerlikon-Bührle KDC L/90 anti-aircraft guns in two Oerlikon-Bührle GDM-A twin mountings

Missile armament: Two twin container-launchers for four Aérospatiale MM.38 Exocet anti-ship missiles

Torpedo armament: Two single 21in (533mm) mountings for two AEG SST-4 wire-guided heavyweight anti-ship torpedoes

Anti-submarine armament: None

Electronics: One Thomson-CSF Triton surface-search radar, one Decca 1226C navigation radar, one Thomson-CSF Pollux tracking radar used in conjunction with one Thomson-CSF Vega fire-control system, and one Plessey Mk 10 IFF system

Propulsion: Diesel arrangement with four MTU 16V 538 diesel engines delivering a total of 11,990hp (8,940kW) to four shafts

Performance: Maximum speed 36.5kt; range 2,300 miles (3,700km) at 15kt or 980 miles (1,575km) at 25kt

Complement: 4+36

Germany ("Type 148" class)			
Name	*No.*	*Builder*	*Commissioned*
Tiger	P6141	CMN, Cherbourg	Oct 1972
Iltis	P6142	CMN, Cherbourg	Jan 1973
Luchs	P6143	CMN, Cherbourg	Apr 1973
Marder	P6144	CMN, Cherbourg	Jun 1973
Leopard	P6145	CMN, Cherbourg	Aug 1973
Fuchs	P6146	Lürssen/CMN	Oct 1973
Jaguar	P6147	CMN, Cherbourg	Nov 1973
Löwe	P6148	Lürssen/CMN	Jan 1974
Wolf	P6149	CMN, Cherbourg	Feb 1974
Panther	P6150	Lürssen/CMN	Mar 1974
Häher	P6151	CMN, Cherbourg	Jun 1974
Storch	P6152	Lürssen/CMN	Jul 1974
Pelikan	P6153	CMN, Cherbourg	Sep 1974
Elster	P6154	Lürssen/CMN	Nov 1974
Alk	P6155	CMN, Cherbourg	Jan 1975
Dommel	P6156	Lürssen/CMN	Feb 1975
Weihe	P6157	CMN, Cherbourg	Apr 1975
Pinguin	P6158	Lürssen/CMN	May 1975
Reiher	P6159	CMN, Cherbourg	Jun 1975
Kranich	P6160	Lürssen/CMN	Aug 1975

Notes

These German craft are derivatives of the basic "La Combattante II" class design, and were ordered in December 1970 from the French Direction Technique de Constructions Navales, although eight hulls were completed by Lürssen for fitting-out in France. The craft are FAC(M/G)s, and have standard and full-load displacements of 234 and 265 tons on dimensions that include a length of 152ft 3in (47.0m), beam of 24ft 11in (7.6m) and draught of 8ft 3in (2.5m). The armament consists of one 76mm (3in) OTO Melara dual-purpose gun in an OTO Melara Compact single mounting and one 40mm Bofors L/70 anti-aircraft gun in a Bofors single mounting, plus two twin container-launchers for four MM.38 Exocet anti-ship missiles; if the 40mm gun is removed, two minelaying rails can be installed. The sensors include one Triton G air/surface-search radar, one 3RM 20 navigation radar and one Castor tracking radar used in conjunction with one Vega fire-control system, and other electronic features include one Panda optical director, one Link 11 data-link, one Racal ESM system with warning and jamming elements, and one IFF system. The powerplant comprises four MTU 872 diesel engines delivering a total of 14,405hp (10,470kW) to four shafts for a maximum speed of 36kt and a range of 700 miles (1,125km) at 30kt. The complement is 4+26.

Pelikan was produced as the 13th unit of the German navy's 20-strong "Type 148" class variant of the "La Combattante II" class of FAC(M)s built in France and Germany. The basic German standard includes a 3in (76mm) OTO Melara dual-purpose gun forward and a 40mm Bofors gun (classified as an anti-aircraft weapon but in fact a dual-purpose type) aft together with two twin container-launchers for Exocet anti-ship missiles arranged to fire obliquely forward and outboard from locations abaft the super-structure.

Greece (Haulk class)

Name	No.	Builder	Commissioned
Anthipoploiarhos Anninos	P14	CMN, Cherbourg	Jun 1972
Ipoploiarhos Arliotis	P15	CMN, Cherbourg	Apr 1972
Ipoploiarhos Konidis	P16	CMN, Cherbourg	Jul 1972
Ipoploiarhos Batsis	P17	CMN, Cherbourg	Dec 1971

Notes

These craft were ordered in 1969, and all four units were modernised by the early 1990s.

Iran ("Kaman" class)

Name	No.	Builder	Commissioned
Kaman	P221	CMN, Cherbourg	Aug 1977
Zoubin	P222	CMN, Cherbourg	Sep 1977
Khadang	P223	CMN, Cherbourg	Mar 1978
Falakhon	P226	CMN, Cherbourg	Mar 1978
Shamshir	P227	CMN, Cherbourg	Mar 1978
Gorz	P228	CMN, Cherbourg	Aug 1978
Gardouneh	P229	CMN, Cherbourg	Sep 1978
Khanjar	P230	CMN, Cherbourg	Aug 1981
Heyzeh	P231	CMN, Cherbourg	Aug 1981
Tabarzin	P232	CMN, Cherbourg	Aug 1981

The Ipoploiarhos Konidis was built in France as the third of the Greek navy's four "La Combattante II" class FAC(M/T)s. All four of the craft were extensively refurbished and updated in the 1990s for continued viability. The class operates mainly in the Aegean Sea, where the number of islands offers an ideal operational scenario for FACs.

Notes

These Iranian FAC(M/G)s were ordered in two equal batches during February and October 1974, and are similar in hull and machinery to the Greek units although with a different armament and electronic fit. The armament comprises one 76mm (3in) OTO Melara L/62 OTO Melara dual-purpose gun in an OTO Melara Compact single mounting, one 40mm Bofors L/70 anti-aircraft gun in a Breda single mounting, and two twin container-launchers for four McDonnell Douglas RGM-84 Harpoon anti-ship missiles used in conjunction with a WM-28 gun and SSM fire-control system. The Iranians received only 12 Harpoon missiles before the imposition of an American embargo after the fall of the Shah in 1979, and the last three craft were not fitted with Harpoon launchers. The propulsion comprises four MTU 16V 538 TB91 diesel engines delivering 14,405hp (10,740kW), and with a full-load displacement of 275 tons the maximum speed is 34.5kt, with a range of 2,300 miles (3,700km) at 15kt declining to 805 miles (1,300km) at 33.7kt. A complement of 31 is carried. The eleventh and twelfth units of the class, *Peykan* and *Joshan*, were sunk in combat, the former by the Iraqis during 1980 in the Gulf War, and the latter by US forces in April 1988.

Libya ("La Combattante IIG" class)

Name	No.	Builder	Commissioned
Sharara	518	CMN, Cherbourg	Feb 1982
Wahag	522	CMN, Cherbourg	May 1982
Shehab	524	CMN, Cherbourg	Apr 1982
Shouaiai	528	CMN, Cherbourg	Sep 1982
Shoula	532	CMN, Cherbourg	Oct 1982
Shafak	534	CMN, Cherbourg	Dec 1982
Bark	536	CMN, Cherbourg	Mar 1983
Rad	538	CMN, Cherbourg	May 1983
Laheeb	542	CMN, Cherbourg	Jul 1983

Notes

These Libyan FAC(M/G)s were ordered in May 1977 to an enlarged "La Combattante II" design with standard and full-load displacements of 258 and 311 tons respectively on dimensions that include a length of 162ft 1in (49.4m), beam of 23ft 4in (7.1m) and draught of 6ft 7in (2.0m). The missile armament comprises four single container-launchers for four OTO Melara/Matra Otomat anti-ship missiles, and the other weapons include one 76mm (3in) OTO Melara L/62 dual-purpose gun in an OTO Melara Compact single

mounting and two 40mm Bofors L/70 anti-aircraft guns in a Breda twin mounting. The electronics fit is one Triton surface-search radar, one Castor I tracking radar used in conjunction with one Vega II fire-control system, and one Panda optical director. The powerplant of four MTU 20V 538 TB91 diesel engines delivers a total of 18,000hp (13,420kW) to four shafts for a maximum speed of 39kt and a range of 1,840 miles (2,960km) at 15kt. The complement is 27. A tenth unit, *Waheed* (526), was sunk by US forces in March 1986, and a second "La Combattante IIG" class unit was severely damaged two days later.

Malaysia
("La Combattante IID" or "Perdana" class)

Name	No.	Builder	Commissioned
Perdana	3501	CMN, Cherbourg	Dec 1972
Serang	3502	CMN, Cherbourg	Jan 1973
Ganas	3503	CMN, Cherbourg	Feb 1973
Ganyang	3504	CMN, Cherbourg	Mar 1973

Notes

Ordered in 1970, these Malaysian FAC(M/G)s are close to the norm in displacement and dimensions. The missile armament comprises two single container-launchers for two MM.38 Exocet anti-ship missiles, and the other weapons include one 57mm Bofors SAK 57 Mk I L/70 dual-purpose gun in a Bofors single mounting and one 40mm Bofors L/70 anti-aircraft gun in a Bofors single mounting. The electronic suite includes one Triton surface-search radar, one Decca 616 navigation radar, one Pollux tracking radar used in conjunction with one Vega fire-control system, one ESM system with warning element, and four 57mm chaff/flare launchers. The powerplant of four MTU 870 diesel engines delivers a total of 13,950hp (10,400kW) to four shafts for a maximum speed of 36.5kt and a range of 930 miles (1,500km) at 25kt. The complement is 5+30.

This is one of the Libyan navy's original force of 10 "La Combattante IIG" class FAC(M/G)s, of which one was sunk by US naval forces in March 1986.

"La Combattante III" class
(France/Greece)

Type: Fast attack craft (missile and gun)

Displacement: 359 tons standard and 425 tons full load (P20-P23) or 329 tons standard and 429 tons full load (P24-P29)

Dimensions: Length 184ft 0in (56.2m); beam 26ft 3in (8.0m); draught 7ft 0in (2.1m)

Gun armament: Two 76mm (3in) OTO Melara L/62 dual-purpose guns in OTO Melara Compact single mountings, and four 30mm Oerlikon-Bührle KCB L/85 anti-aircraft guns in two EMERLEC-30 twin mountings

Missile armament: Four container-launchers for four Aérospatiale MM.38 Exocet anti-ship missiles, or (P24-P29) six container-launchers for six Kongsberg Penguin Mk II anti-ship missiles

Torpedo armament: Two single 21in (533mm) mountings for two AEG SST-4 wire-guided anti-ship torpedoes (in P20-P23 only)

Anti-submarine armament: None

Electronics: One Thomson-CSF Triton surface-search radar, one Decca 1226 navigation radar, one Thomson-CSF Castor II tracking radar and one Thomson-CSF Pollux tracking radar used in conjunction with one Thomson-CSF Vega I or II fire-control system, and two Thomson-CSF Panda optical directors

Propulsion: Diesel arrangement with four MTU 20V 538 TB92 diesel engines delivering a total of 20,780hp (15,500kW) in P20-P23, or four MTU 20V 538 TB91 diesel engines delivering a total of 15,020hp (11,200kW) in P24-P29, in each case to four shafts

Performance: Maximum speed 35.7kt in P20-P23, or 32.5kt in P24-P29; range 2,300 miles (3,700km) at 15kt or 810 miles (1,300km) at 32.6kt

Complement: 5+37

Greece (La Combattante III class)			
Name	No.	Builder	Commissioned
Antiploiarhos Laskos	P20	CMN, Cherbourg	Apr 1977
Plotarhis Blessas	P21	CMN, Cherbourg	Jul 1977
Ipoploiarhos Mikonios	P22	CMN, Cherbourg	Feb 1978
Ipoploiarhos Troupakis	P23	CMN, Cherbourg	Nov 1977
Simeoforos Kavaloudis	P24	Hellenic Shipyards	Jul 1980
Anthipoploiarhos Kostakos	P25	Hellenic Shipyards	Sep 1980
Ipoploiarhos Deyiannis	P26	Hellenic Shipyards	Dec 1980
Simeoforos Xenos	P27	Hellenic Shipyards	Mar 1981
Simeoforos Simitzopoulos	P28	Hellenic Shipyards	Jun 1981
Simeoforos Starakis	P29	Hellenic Shipyards	Oct 1981

Notes

These impressive FAC(M/G)s fall into two subclasses. Ordered in September 1974, the four craft built in France have fewer anti-ship missiles but have two anti-ship torpedoes and higher performance, while the six licence-built in Greece (after an order placed in 1977) have more anti-ship missiles but no torpedoes, and lower performance.

Nigeria ("La Combattante IIIB" class)			
Name	No.	Builder	Commissioned
Siri	P181	CMN, Cherbourg	Feb 1981
Ayam	P182	CMN, Cherbourg	Jun 1981
Ekun	P183	CMN, Cherbourg	Sep 1981

Notes

Ordered in November 1977 as potent FAC(M/G)s, these Nigerian craft are named "tiger" in the three main Nigerian languages, and have standard and full-load displacements of

Lead vessel of the six-strong second subvariant of the Greek navy's 10-strong "La Combattante III" class of FAC(M/G)s, the Simeoforos Kavaloudis was the first of the class built in a Greek rather than French yard. The subvariant is powerfully armed with two 3in (76mm) OTO Melara dual-purpose guns, four 35 mm cannon on the rear of the forward superstructure block, six container-launchers for Penguin anti-ship missiles and, in a trial installation typical of the first four craft but not the last six, two rearward-firing 21in (533mm) tubes for wire-guided heavyweight anti-ship torpedoes.

385 and 430 tons respectively on dimensions that include a length of 184ft 5in (56.2m), beam of 24ft 11in (7.6m) and draught of 7ft 0in (2.1m). The missile armament comprises two twin container-launchers for four Aérospatiale MM.38 Exocet anti-ship missiles, and the other weapons consist of one 76mm (3in) OTO Melara L/62 dual-purpose gun in an OTO Melara Compact single mounting (250 rounds), two 40mm Bofors L/70 anti-aircraft guns in a Breda twin mounting (1,600 rounds), and four 30mm Oerlikon-Bührle KCB L/85 anti-aircraft guns in two EMERLEC-30 twin mountings (1,970 rounds). The electronics suite includes one Triton surface-search radar, one Decca 1226 navigation radar and one Castor II tracking radar used in conjunction with one Vega fire-control system; other features are two Panda optical directors and one ESM system with RDL-2 warning element. The propulsion arrangement comprises four MTU 16V 956 TB92 diesel engines delivering a total of 20,840hp (15,540kW) to four shafts for a maximum speed of 41kt and a range of 2,300 miles (3,700km) at 15kt. The complement is 42.

Qatar ("La Combattante IIIM" class)

Name	No.	Builder	Commissioned
Damsah	Q01	CMN, Cherbourg	Nov 1982
Al Ghariyah	Q02	CMN, Cherbourg	Feb 1983
Rbigah	Q03	CMN, Cherbourg	May 1983

Notes

Ordered in October 1980, these Qatari craft are similar to the Tunisian units in all essential respects.

Tunisia ("La Combattante IIIM" class)

Name	No.	Builder	Commissioned
La Galit	501	CMN, Cherbourg	Oct 1984
Tunis	502	CMN, Cherbourg	Nov 1984
Carthage	503	CMN, Cherbourg	Dec 1984

Notes

Ordered in August 1981 with French funding and generally similar to the Greek units, these Tunisian FAC(M/G)s have a beam enlarged to 26ft 11in (8.2m) for standard and full-load displacements of 345 and 425 tons respectively. The missile armament comprises two quadruple container-launchers for eight MM.40 Exocet anti-ship missiles, and the other weapons consist of one 76mm (3in) OTO Melara L/62 dual-purpose gun in an OTO Melara Compact single mounting, two 40mm Bofors L/70 anti-aircraft guns in a Breda twin mounting, and two 30mm Oerlikon-Bührle KCB L/75 anti-aircraft guns in an Oerlikon-Bührle GCM-A03 twin mounting. Amongst the electronics fit are one Triton surface-search radar, one Castor II tracking radar used in conjunction with one Vega II fire-control system, one Sylosat satellite navigation system, two Naja optronic directors, one ESM system with warning element, and one CSEE Dagaie chaff/flare launcher. The propulsion system comprises four MTU 20V 538 TB93 diesel engines delivering a total of 19,315hp (14,400kW) to four shafts for a maximum speed of 38.5kt and a range of 3,230 miles (5,200km) at 18kt declining to 810 miles (1,300km) at 33kt. The complement is 35.

"Lürssen FPB-36" class
(Germany/Mauritania)

Type: Fast attack craft (gun)

Displacement: 139 tons full load

Dimensions: Length 118ft 9in (36.2m); beam 19ft 0in (5.8m); draught 6ft 3in (1.9m)

Gun armament: One 40mm Bofors L/70 anti-aircraft gun in a single mounting, one 20mm Hispano-Suiza HS-804 L/75 anti-aircraft gun in an Oerlikon-Bührle A41A single mounting, and two 0.5in (12.7mm) Browning M2 machine-guns in single mountings

Missile armament: None

Torpedo armament: None

Anti-submarine armament: None

Electronics: One Raytheon RN 1220/6XB surface-search radar, and one Panda optical director

Propulsion: Diesel arrangement with two MTU 16V 538 TB90 diesel engines delivering a total of 5,765hp (4,300kW) to two shafts

Performance: Maximum speed 36kt; range 1,385 miles (2,225km) at 17kt

Complement: 3+16

This overhead view of the Guacolda, lead unit of the Chilean navy's four-strong variant of the "Lürssen FPB-36" class of FAC(T)s built in the yard of the parent company's Spanish licensee, reveals the salient deck layout of this useful but comparatively simple variant.

Chile ("Guacolda" class)

Name	No.	Builder	Commissioned
Guacolda	80	Bazan	Jul 1965
Fresia	81	Bazan	Dec 1965
Quidora	82	Bazan	Mar 1966
Tegualda	83	Bazan	Jul 1966

Notes

Ordered in 1963, these FAC(T)s may be regarded as the precursors of the "Lürssen FPB-36" type, with a full-load displacement of 134 tons on dimensions that include a length of 118ft 1in (36.0m), beam of 18ft 4in (5.6m) and draught of 7ft 3in (2.2m). The armament is two 40mm Bofors L/60 anti-aircraft guns in Bofors single mountings and four single 21in (533mm) British Mk 4 mountings for heavyweight anti-ship torpedoes. The electronics fit is limited to one Decca 505 surface-search and navigation radar, and propulsion is entrusted to two Mercedes-Benz MB 839Bd diesel engines delivering a total of 4,830hp (3,600kW) to two shafts for a maximum speed of 32kt and a range of 1,740 miles (2,800km) at 15kt. The complement is 20.

Congo ("Guacolda" class)

Name	No.	Builder	Commissioned
Marien N'Gouabi	P601	Bazan	Nov 1982
Les Trois Glorieuses	P602	Bazan	Jan 1983
Les Maloango	P603	Bazan	Mar 1983

Notes

Ordered in 1980, these are simple patrol craft derived from the "Barcelo" class. The displacement, dimensions, propulsion arrangement and performance differ slightly from the Spanish norm, and the armament comprises one 40mm Bofors L/70 anti-aircraft gun in a Breda single mounting, one 20mm Oerlikon-Bührle anti-aircraft gun in a single mounting and two 0.5in (12.7mm) machine-guns in single mountings, and this armament is used in conjunction with one Decca surface-search and navigation radar and one Panda optical director.

Ecuador ("Manta" class)

Name	No.	Builder	Commissioned
Manta	LM27	Lürssen	Jun 1971
Tulcan	LM28	Lürssen	Apr 1971
Nuevo Rocafuerte	LM29	Lürssen	Jun 1971

Notes

This is an FAC(M) variant of the "Guacolda" class with upgraded electronics and an additional engine driving a third shaft for higher performance. The standard and full-load displacements are 119 and 134 tons respectively on dimensions that include a length of 119ft 5in (36.4m), beam of 19ft 1in (5.8m) and draught of 6ft 0in (1.8m). Each of the three craft was originally armed with one 40mm Bofors L/70 anti-aircraft gun in a single mounting and two single 21in (533mm) mountings for heavyweight anti-ship torpedoes, but the class was rearmed in 1979 with smaller-calibre guns and in 1981 with anti-ship missiles. The missile armament comprises four single container-launchers for four IAI Gabriel II anti-ship missiles, and the other component of the weapon system is four 30mm Oerlikon-Bührle KCB L/85 anti-aircraft guns in two EMERLEC-30 twin mountings. The electronics fit comprises one navigation radar and one Pollux tracking radar used in conjunction with one Vega fire-control system. The propulsion arrangement comprises three Mercedes-Benz MB 839Bd diesel engines delivering a total of 9,055hp (6,750kW) to three shafts for a maximum speed of 42kt and a range of 1,740 miles (2,800km) at 15kt declining to 805 miles (1,300km) at 30kt. The complement is 19.

Mauritania			
Name	No.	Builder	Commissioned
El Vaiz	P361	Bazan	Oct 1979
El Beig	P362	Bazan	May 1979
El Kinz	P363	Bazan	Aug 1982

Notes
These are small and wholly unexceptional FAC(G)s limited in practical use to patrol and training. The first two units

These three units of the Chilean navy's "Guacolda" class are seen in typical operating conditions in the Beagle Channel near the extreme southern tip of South America.

were ordered in 1976, and the third in 1979. Mauritania had planned to order another three of this type, which is very similar to the Spanish "Barcelo" class, but the crisis caused by the independence of the Spanish Sahara led the country to plan more ambitious light forces.

Spain ("Barcelo" class)

Name	No.	Builder	Commissioned
Barcelo	P11	Lürssen	Mar 1976
Laya	P12	Bazan	Dec 1976
Javier Quiroga	P13	Bazan	Apr 1977
Ordonez	P14	Bazan	Jun 1977
Acevedo	P15	Bazan	Jul 1977
Candido Perez	P16	Bazan	Nov 1977

Notes

These are simple FAC(G)s that were ordered in December 1973. The type has a full-load displacement of 134 tons on dimensions that include a length of 118ft 9in (36.2m), beam of 19ft 0in (5.8m) and draught of 6ft 3in (1.9m). The armament comprises one 40mm Bofors L/70 anti-aircraft gun in a Breda single mounting, two 20mm Oerlikon-Bührle KAA L/85 anti-aircraft guns in two Oerlikon-Bührle GAM-B01 single mountings and two 0.5in (12.7mm) machine-guns in single mountings; each craft is fitted for (but not with) two single 21in (533mm) mountings for heavyweight anti-ship torpedoes, and two or four container-launchers for two or four anti-ship missiles in place of the torpedo tubes and 20mm cannon. The electronics fit includes one Raytheon 1220/6XB surface-search radar and one Panda optical director. The propulsion arrangement is based on two Bazan-built MTU 16V 538 TB90 diesel engines delivering a total of 5,765hp (4,300kW) to two shafts for a maximum speed of 36kt and a range of 1,385 miles (2,225km) at 17kt. The complement is 3+16.

"Lürssen FPB-38" class
(Germany/Bahrain)

Type: Fast attack craft (gun)

Displacement: 188 tons standard and 205 tons full load

Dimensions: Length 126ft 4in (38.5m); beam 22ft 11in (7.0m); draught 7ft 3in (2.2m)

Gun armament: Two 40mm Bofors L/70 anti-aircraft guns in a Breda Compact twin mounting, two 20mm Oerlikon-Bührle KAA L/85 anti-aircraft guns in two Oerlikon-Bührle GAM-B01 single mountings, and two 7.62mm (0.3in) machine-guns in single mountings

Missile armament: None

Torpedo armament: None

Anti-submarine armament: None

Mines: Two rails fitted for 14 mines

Electronics: One Bofors Electronics 9GR 600 surface-search and fire-control radar, one Decca 1226 navigation radar, one CSEE Lynx optronic director used in conjunction with one Bofors Electronics 9LV 100 fire-control system, and one CSEE Dagaie chaff launcher

Propulsion: Diesel arrangement with two MTU 20V 539 TB91 diesel engines delivering a total of 8,985hp (6,700kW) to two shafts

Performance: Maximum speed 33kt; range 1,245 miles (2,000km) at 16kt or 685 miles (1,100km) at 30.5kt

Complement: 3+16 plus provision for 2 spare officers

Bahrain (Lürssen FPB-38 class)

Name	No.	Builder	Commissioned
Al Riffa	10	Lürssen	Aug 1981
Hawar	11	Lürssen	Nov 1981

Notes

Ordered in 1979, this is a small FAC(G) type with only limited armament and capabilities. The craft were originally to have been fitted with a single 40mm Bofors L/70 anti-aircraft gun in a single mounting.

Malaysia (Lürssen FPB-38 class)

Name	No.	Builder	Commissioned
		Lürssen	

The Al Riffa is the lead unit of the Bahraini navy's two-strong complement of "Lürssen FPB-38" class FACs intended for the patrol role with an armament of two 40mm Bofors guns in a twin turret.

Notes
This class of light FAC(G)s will eventually total 18, and is designed mainly for the patrol role. The type has a full-load displacement of 221 tons on dimensions that include a length of 126ft 4in (38.5m) and beam of 23ft 0in (7.0m). The armament comprises two 20mm Oerlikon-Bührle KAA L/85 anti-aircraft guns in Oerlikon-Bührle GAM-B01 single mountings and two 7.62mm (0.3in) machine-guns in single mountings. The craft are fitted with surface-search radar, and the fire-control system is of the optical type. The propulsion arrangement comprises two MTU diesel engines delivering a total of 9,870hp (7,360kW) to two shafts for a maximum speed of 34.7kt and a range of 1,385 miles (2,225km) at 24kt declining to 1,095 miles (1,760km) at 32.5kt. The crew is 7+30 plus provision for one spare officer.

United Arab Emirates (Abu Dhabi) (Lürssen FPB-38 class)			
Name	No.	Builder	Commissioned
		Lürssen	
		Lürssen	

Notes
These two craft incorporate the general configuration and capabilities of the class.

"Lürssen TNC-42" class
(Germany/Greece)

Type: Fast attack craft (torpedo)

Displacement: 160 tons standard and 190 tons full load

Dimensions: Length 139ft 5in (42.5m); beam 23ft 7in (7.2m); draught 7ft 11in (2.4m)

Gun armament: Two 40mm Bofors L/70 anti-aircraft guns in Bofors single mountings

Missile armament: None

Torpedo armament: Four single 21in (533mm) mountings for four AEG SST-4 wire-guided anti-ship torpedoes

Anti-submarine armament: None

Mines: Up to eight mines in place of torpedo tubes

Electronics: One surface-search and navigation radar

Propulsion: Diesel arrangement with four MTU 16V 538 diesel engines delivering a total of 14,350hp (10,700kW) to four shafts

Performance: Maximum speed 42kt; range 1,150 miles (1,850km) at 32kt or 575 miles (925km) at 40kt

Complement: 39

Greece (Lürssen TNC-42 class)

Name	No.	Builder	Commissioned
Hesperos	P50	Lürssen	Aug 1958
Kentauros	P52	Kröger	Nov 1958
Kyklon	P53	Lürssen	Mar 1959
Lelaps	P54	Lürssen	Feb 1959
Skorpios	P55	Kröger	Nov 1959
Tyfon	P56	Lürssen	Jun 1959

Notes

These obsolete craft are the survivors of 40 "Jaguar" class FAC(T)s built by Lürssen (30 craft) and Kröger (10 craft), all of which have now been deleted or transferred to friendly navies. These Greek craft were transferred from West Germany in 1976 and 1977, together with three others to be cannibalised for spares.

Saudi Arabia (Lürssen TNC-42 class)

Name	No.	Builder	Commissioned
Dammam		Lürssen	1969
Khabar		Lürssen	1969
Maccah		Lürssen	1969

Notes

These craft were ordered by West Germany during 1968, and served in the North Sea and the Baltic until transferred in 1976 after extensive refitting in West German yards. The craft each have a complement of 3+30. Although they have a torpedo capability against surface ships, the craft are used mainly for patrol and training.

Turkey (Lürssen TNC-42 class)

Name	No.	Builder	Commissioned
Mizrak	P333	Lürssen	1962
Kalkan	P335	Lürssen	1959

Notes

These are the survivors of seven "Jaguar" class craft

Now lost, the Meltem was a "Kartal" class FAC(M/T) of the Turkish navy.

transferred from West Germany between late 1976 and early 1977 as operational craft, together with another three non-operational craft to be cannibalised for spares.

Turkey (Kartal class)

Name	No.	Builder	Commissioned
Denizkusu	P321	Lürssen	1967
Atmaca	P322	Lürssen	1967
Sahin	P323	Lürssen	1967
Kartal	P324	Lürssen	1967
Pelikan	P326	Lürssen	1968
Albatros	P327	Lürssen	1968
Simsek	P328	Lürssen	1968
Kasirga	P329	Lürssen	1967

Notes

The "Kartal" FAC(M/T) class is a variant of the "Jaguar" class produced for the Turkish navy. The type has standard and full-load displacements of 160 and 190 tons respectively on dimensions that include a length of 140ft 6in (42.8m), beam of 23ft 6in (7.1m) and draught of 7ft 3in (2.2m). The armament is fairly impressive, comprising four single container-launchers for four Kongsberg Penguin Mk II anti-ship missiles, two 40mm Bofors L/70 anti-aircraft guns in single mountings, and four single 21in (533mm) mountings for heavyweight anti-ship torpedoes. The primary electronic systems are one Decca 1226 surface-search and navigation radar and one tracking radar used in conjunction with one Hollandse Signaalapparaten WM-28 fire-control system. The propulsion arrangement of four MTU 16V 538 diesel engines delivers a total of 11,990hp (8,940kW) to four shafts for a maximum speed of 42kt and a range of 525 miles (925km) at 40kt. The complement is 39. A ninth unit, *Meltem*, sank after collision with a Soviet ship in 1985, and although salvaged was deemed too badly damaged for economic repair.

"Lürssen FPB/TNC-45" class
(Germany/United Arab Emirates)

Type: Fast attack craft (missile and gun)

Displacement: 235 tons standard and 260 tons full load

Dimensions: Length 147ft 4in (44.9m); beam 23ft 0in (7.0m); draught 8ft 3in (2.5m)

Gun armament: One 76mm (3in) OTO Melara L/62 dual-purpose gun in an OTO Melara Compact single mounting, two 40mm Bofors L/70 anti-aircraft guns in a Breda Compact twin mounting, and two 7.62mm (0.3in) machine-guns in single mountings

Missile armament: Two twin container-launchers for four Aérospatiale MM.40 Exocet anti-ship missiles

Torpedo armament: None

Anti-submarine armament: None

Electronics: One Decca TM1226 surface-search and navigation radar, one Bofors Electronics 9LV 200 Mk 2 tracking radar used in conjunction with one Bofors Electronics 9LV 223 fire-control system, one USFA optronic director, one CSEE Panda optical director, one ESM system with Cutlass-E warning and Cygnus jamming elements, and one CSEE Dagaie chaff/flare launcher

Propulsion: Diesel arrangement with four MTU 16V 538 TB92 diesel engines delivering a total of 15,395hp (11,480kW) to four shafts

Performance: Maximum speed 41.4kt; range 1,740 miles (2,800km) at 16kt on two engines or 575 miles (925km) at 38.5kt on four engines

Complement: 5+35 plus provision for 3 spare men

Argentina (Lürssen FPB/TNC-45 class)

Name	No.	Builder	Commissioned
Intrepida	P85	Lürssen	Jul 1974
Indomita	P86	Lürssen	Dec 1974

Notes

Ordered in 1970, these Argentine craft are FAC(G/T)s. The design is moderately different from that of later "FPB/TNC-45" craft, with slightly increased length and beam. The normal and full-load displacements are 240 and 268 tons respectively on dimensions that include a length of 149ft 0in (45.4m), beam of 24ft 3in (7.4m) and draught of 7ft 6in (2.3m). The armament consists of one 76mm (3in) OTO Melara L/62 dual-purpose gun in an OTO Melara Compact single mounting and two 40mm Bofors L/70 anti-aircraft guns in Bofors single mountings, complemented by two single 21in (533mm) mountings for AEG SST-4 wire-guided heavyweight anti-ship torpedoes; each craft is also fitted with two 3.2in (81mm) launchers for illuminants. The

electronics fit includes one Decca 12 navigation radar, one Hollandse Signaalapparaten WM-22 optronic gun fire-control system, one Hollandse Signaalapparaten WM-11 torpedo fire-control system, and one ESM system with warning element. The propulsion arrangement comprises four MTU MD 872 diesel engines delivering a total of 13,950hp (10,400kW) to four shafts for a maximum speed of 40kt and a range of 1,680 miles (2,700km) at 20kt. The complement is 2+37. It had been planned to procure another two units of the same class, but the relevant financial commitment was delayed and then abandoned.

Bahrain (Lürssen FPB/TNC-45 class)

Name	No.	Builder	Commissioned
Ahmed el Fateh	20	Lürssen	Feb 1983
Al Jabiri	21	Lürssen	May 1984
Abdul Rahman al Fadel	22	Lürssen	Sep 1986
Al Taweelah	23	Lürssen	1988

The Al Boom was lead unit of the Kuwaiti navy's six-strong force of "Lürssen TNC-45" class FAC(M/G)s, and was one of the five seized by the Iraqi invaders of Kuwait in 1990 and then either sunk or damaged beyond repair.

Notes

These Bahraini craft are standard FAC(M/G)s basically similar to the UAE craft. The standard and full-load displacements are 228 and 259 tons respectively on dimensions that include a length of 147ft 4in (44.9m), beam of 23ft 0in (7.0m) and draught of 8ft 3in (2.5m). The missile armament comprises two twin container-launchers for four Aérospatiale MM.40 Exocet anti-ship missiles, and the other weapons are one 76mm (3in) OTO Melara L/62 dual-purpose gun in an OTO Melara Compact single mounting (250 rounds), two 40mm Bofors L/70B anti-aircraft guns in a Breda Compact twin mounting (1,800 rounds), and three 7.62mm (0.3in) machine-guns in single mountings (6,000 rounds). The electronics fit includes one Bofors Electronics 9LV 200 surface-search and tracking radar used in conjunction with one Bofors Electronics 9LV 223 fire-control system, one Decca 1226 navigation radar, one CSEE Panda optical director for the 40mm guns, one ESM system with Cutlass-E warning and RDL-2ABC jamming elements, and one CSEE Dagaie chaff/flare launcher. The propulsion arrangement comprises four MTU 16V 538 TB92 diesel engines delivering a total of 15,395hp (11,480kW) to four shafts for a maximum speed of 41.5kt and a range of 1,740 miles (2,800km) at 16kt on two engines, declining to 575 miles (925km) at 38.5kt. The first pair of craft was ordered in 1979, while the slightly different second pair was ordered in 1985. These craft each have a beam of 23ft 11in (7.3m) and engines delivering a total of 15,560hp (11,600kW) for a maximum speed of 42kt. A third pair of boats was ordered in 1986 to the revised standard of the second pair, but it is thought that these two craft were later cancelled. The complement is 6+30 plus provision for 3 spare men.

Chile (Lürssen FPB/TNC-45 class)

Name	No.	Builder	Commissioned
Iquique	32	CMN, Cherbourg	1969
Covadonga	33	CMN, Cherbourg	1969

Notes

These Chilean FAC(M/G)s are the ex-Israeli "Saar 3" class craft *Hanit* and *Hetz* sold to Chile in December 1988. The armament comprises six single container-launchers for six

The Israeli navy has been one of the major operators of the "Lürssen TNC-45" class of FAC(M/G)s for some time, originally receiving 12 craft in two equal-size "Saar" classes.

IAI Gabriel II anti-ship missiles, one 76mm (3in) OTO Melara L/62 dual-purpose gun in an OTO Melara Compact single mounting, and two 20mm Oerlikon-Bührle anti-aircraft guns in single mountings.

Ecuador (Lürssen FPB/TNC-45 class)

Name	No.	Builder	Commissioned
Quito	LM21	Lürssen	Jul 1976
Guayaquil	LM23	Lürssen	Dec 1977
Cuenca	LM24	Lürssen	Jul 1977

Notes

Ordered in the early 1970s, these Ecuadorian FAC(M/G)s approximate closely to the norm at standard and full-load displacements of 250 and 265 tons respectively on dimensions that include a length of 147ft 8in (45.0m), beam of 23ft 0in (7.0m) and draught of 8ft 3in (2.5m). The missile armament comprises four single container-launchers for four Aérospatiale MM.38 Exocet anti-ship missiles, and the other weapons consist of one 76mm (3in) OTO Melara L/62 dual-purpose gun in an OTO Melara Compact single mounting and two 35mm Oerlikon-Bührle KDC L/90 anti-aircraft guns in an Oerlikon-Bührle GDM-A twin mounting. The electronics fit includes one Thomson-CSF Triton air/surface-search radar, one Decca navigation radar, and one Thomson-CSF Pollux tracking radar used in conjunction with one Thomson-CSF Vega fire-control system. The propulsion arrangement comprises four MTU 16V 538 diesel engines delivering a total of 13,950hp (10,400kW) to four shafts for a maximum speed of 40kt and a range of 2,080 miles (3,350km) at 16kt declining to 810 miles (1,300km) at 40kt. The complement is 35.

Ghana (Lürssen FPB/TNC-45 class)

Name	No.	Builder	Commissioned
Dzata	P26	Lürssen	Jul 1980
Sebo	P27	Lürssen	Jul 1980

Notes

Ordered in 1976, these Ghanaian craft are FAC(G)s with a full-load displacement of 269 tons on dimensions that include a length of 147ft 4in (44.9m), beam of 23ft 0in (7.0m) and draught of 8ft 11in (2.7m). The armament, originally consisting of one 76mm (3in) OTO Melara L/62 dual-purpose gun in an OTO Melara Compact single mounting and one 40mm Bofors L/70 anti-aircraft gun in a single mounting, has been revised to two 40mm Bofors L/70 anti-aircraft guns in single mountings to suit the craft for their current fishery protection role. The electronic fit includes one surface-search radar used in conjunction with one Thomson-CSF Canopus A fire-control system, one Decca Type 978 navigation radar, and one LIOD optronic director. The propulsion arrangement of two MTU 16V 538 TB91 diesel engines delivers a total of 7,110hp (5,300kW) to two shafts for a maximum speed of 29.5kt and a range of

3,320 miles (4,450km) at 15kt declining to 1,275 miles (2,050km) at 25kt. The complement is 5+30 with a maximum of 55 possible.

Israel ("Saar 2" or "Mivtach" class)			
Name	No.	Builder	Commissioned
Mivtach	311	CMN, Cherbourg	1968
Miznag	312	CMN, Cherbourg	1968
Mifgav	313	CMN, Cherbourg	1968
Eilath	321	CMN, Cherbourg	1968
Haifa	322	CMN, Cherbourg	1968
Akko	323	CMN, Cherbourg	1968

Notes

Ordered in 1965, these Israeli FAC(M/G)s were built in France to avoid the political problems that would have followed construction in West Germany, and are exceptionally well equipped. As originally fitted out, the craft were "Saar 1" class FAC(G)s with an armament of three 40mm Bofors L/70 anti-aircraft guns in single Breda 58/11 mountings, two 0.5in (12.7mm) Browning machine-guns in single mountings and four single 12.75in (324mm) Mk 32 mountings for Mk 46 anti-submarine torpedoes, but were then upgraded to the present impressive "Saar 2" class configuration. The standard and full-load displacements are 220 and 250 tons respectively on dimensions that include a length of 147ft 8in (45.0m), beam of 23ft 0in (7.0m) and draught of 8ft 3in (2.5m). The missile armament comprises between two and eight container-launchers for between two and eight IAI Gabriel II anti-ship missiles (two trainable triple container-launchers being fitted on the after ring mountings if only one 40mm gun is carried), while the other weapons consist of between one and three 40mm Bofors L/70 anti-aircraft guns in Breda single mountings, two or four 0.5in (12.7mm) Browning machine-guns in single mountings, and two twin 12.75in (324mm) Mk 32 mountings for Mk 46 anti-submarine torpedoes if no triple missile container-launcher units are shipped. The electronic fit includes one Thomson-CSF TH-D 1040 Neptune air/surface-search radar, one Selenia Orion RTN 10X tracking radar used in conjunction with one Selenia Argo

Another "Lurssen TNC-45" class craft of the Kuwaiti navy and seen here in a turn to port, the Al Betteel was one of the five of this class lost or irreparably damaged in 1991.

NA10 fire-control system, one EDO 780 active search and attack variable-depth sonar (not in all craft), one ESM system with an Elta MN-53 warning element and a jamming element, one IAI Reshet data-link system, and a combination of six 24-tube and four single-tube chaff launchers. The propulsion arrangement of four MTU MD 871 diesel engines delivers a total of 13,410hp (10,000kW) to four shafts for a maximum speed of more than 40kt and a range of 2,890 miles (4,650km) at 15kt declining to 1,835 miles (2,950km) at 20kt and finally to 1,150 miles (1,850km) at 30kt. The complement is 5+30/35.

Israel ("Saar 3" class)			
Name	No.	Builder	Commissioned
Soufa	332	CMN, Cherbourg	1969

Notes

Ordered in 1966 as a batch of six FAC(M/G)s of which two have now been transferred to Chile and another three deleted, this class was planned as a variant of the "Saar 1" class with one 76mm (3in) OTO Melara L/62 dual-purpose gun in an OTO Melara compact single mounting and two 40mm Bofors L/70 anti-aircraft guns in single Breda 58/11 mountings, but with no anti-submarine armament because of the weight and volume restrictions imposed by the 76mm (3in) gun. The craft were later upgraded to a standard comparable to that of the "Saar 2" class. The gun armament is centred on one 76mm (3in) OTO Melara L/62 dual-purpose gun located forward in an OTO Melara Compact single mounting, with the option of two 40mm Bofors L/70 anti-aircraft guns or two triple container-launchers for six IAI Gabriel II anti-ship missiles aft.

Kuwait (Lürssen FPB/TNC-45 class)			
Name	No.	Builder	Commissioned
Al Sanbouk	P4505	Lürssen	1983

Notes

In 1980 the Kuwaitis ordered a class of six "Lürssen TNC-45" class craft that were delivered in 1983 and 1984 as four and two vessels respectively. When Iraq invaded Kuwait in 1990, *Al Sanbouk* escaped to Bahrain and the other five craft (*Al Boom, Al Betteel, Al Saadi, Al Ahmadi* and *Al Abdali*) were seized by the Iraqis and either sunk or damaged beyond economic repair in the campaign that ousted the Iraqis from their conquest. This Kuwaiti FAC(M/G) has standard and full-load displacements of 255 and 275 tons respectively on dimensions that include a length of 147ft 4in (44.9m), beam of 23ft 0in (7.0m) and draught of 8ft 10in (2.68m). The missile armament comprises two twin container-launchers for four Aérospatiale MM.40 Exocet anti-ship missiles, and the other weapons consist of one 76mm (3in) OTO Melara L/62 dual-purpose gun in an OTO Melara Compact single mounting, two 40mm Bofors L/70 anti-aircraft guns in a Breda Compact twin mounting, and two 7.62mm (0.3in) machine-guns in single mountings. The electronics fit is one Decca TM 1226C surface-search and navigation radar, one Bofors Electronics 9LV 200 tracking radar used in conjunction with one Bofors Electronics 9LV 228 fire-control system, one CSEE Lynx optical director, one ESM system with Marconi Cutlass-E/Matilda warning element, and one CSEE Dagaie chaff/flare launcher. The propulsion arrangement comprises four MTU 16V 956 TB92 diesel engines delivering a total of 15,560hp (11,600kW) to four shafts for a maximum speed of 41.5kt and a range of 1,925 miles (3,100km) at 16kt on two engines. The complement is 5+30 plus provision for 3 spare men.

Malaysia ("Jerong" class)

Name	No.	Builder	Commissioned
Jerong	3505	Hong-Leong Lürssen	Mar 1976
Todak	3506	Hong-Leong Lürssen	Jun 1976
Paus	3507	Hong-Leong Lürssen	Aug 1976
Yu	3508	Hong-Leong Lürssen	Nov 1976
Baung	3509	Hong-Leong Lürssen	Jan 1977
Pari	3510	Hong-Leong Lürssen	Mar 1977

Notes

Ordered in 1973, these Malaysian craft are FAC(G)s with standard and full-load displacements of 210 and 244 tons respectively on dimensions that include a length of 147ft 4in (44.9m), beam of 23ft 0in (7.0m) and draught of 8ft 2in (2.48m). The armament consists of one 57mm Bofors SAK 57 Mk 1 L/70 dual-purpose gun in a Bofors single mounting, one 40mm Bofors L/70 anti-aircraft gun in a single mounting, and two 7.62mm (0.3in) machine-guns in single mountings. The electronics fit includes one Decca Type 626 surface-search radar, one Kelvin Hughes MS 32 navigation radar, one tracking radar used in conjunction with one Hollandse Signaalapparaten WM-28 fire-control system, one CSEE Naja optronic director and one CSEE Panda optical director. The propulsion arrangement of three MTU MD 872 diesel engines delivers a total of 10,665hp (7,950kW) to three shafts for a maximum speed of 34kt and a range of 2,300 miles (3,700km) at 15kt declining to 810 miles (1,300km) at 31.5kt. The complement is 5+31.

Malaysia (Lürssen FPB/TNC-45 class)

Name	No.	Builder	Commissioned
Sea Wolf	P76	Lürssen	1972
Sea Lion	P77	Lürssen	1972
Sea Dragon	P78	Singapore SB & Eng	1974
Sea Tiger	P79	Singapore SB & Eng	1974
Sea Hawk	P80	Singapore SB & Eng	1975
Sea Scorpion	P81	Singapore SB & Eng	1975

Notes

Ordered in 1970, these Singapore FAC(M/G)s have standard and full-load displacements of 226 and 254 tons respectively on dimensions that include a length of 147ft 4in (44.9m), beam of 23ft 0in (7.0m) and draught of 7ft 6in (2.3m). The missile armament comprises one triple and two single container-launchers for five IAI Gabriel I anti-ship missiles, or two twin container-launchers for four McDonnell Douglas RGM-84 Harpoon anti-ship missiles and two single container-launchers for two Gabriel I anti-ship missiles, and other weapons consist of one 57mm Bofors SAK 57 Mk 1 L/70 dual-purpose gun in a Bofors single mounting (504 rounds) and one 40mm Bofors L/70 anti-aircraft gun in a single mounting (1,008 rounds). The electronics fit includes

one Decca surface-search radar, one Kelvin Hughes 17 navigation radar, one tracking radar used in conjunction with the Hollandse Signaalapparaten WM-28/5 fire-control system, and one Racal ESM system with warning and jamming elements. The propulsion arrangement of four MTU 16V 538 TB92 diesel engines delivers a total of 14,405hp (10,740kW) to four shafts for a maximum speed of 38kt and a range of 2,300 miles (3,700km) at cruising speed. The complement is 5+36. It was for these craft that Israel allowed the first export order for its Gabriel anti-ship missile.

Thailand (Lürssen FPB/TNC-45 class)			
Name	No.	Builder	Commissioned
Prabparapak	1	Singapore SB & Eng	Jul 1976
Hanhak Sattru	2	Singapore SB & Eng	Nov 1976
Suphairin	3	Singapore SB & Eng	Feb 1977

This is a "Lürssen TNC-45" class FAC(M/G) of the Singaporean navy, which operates six of this potently armed subvariant: the gun armament of one 57mm and one 40mm Bofors weapons is complemented here by five Penguin anti-ship missiles (one triple and two single container-launchers) that can be replaced by four Harpoon anti-ship missiles (two twin container-launchers).

Notes

Ordered in June 1973, these Thai FAC(M/G)s are essentially similar to the Singapore units in dimensions, weapons, electronics, propulsion and performance.

United Arab Emirates (Abu Dhabi) (Lürssen FPB/TNC-45 class)

Name	No.	Builder	Commissioned
Ban Yas	P4501	Lürssen	Nov 1980
Marban	P4502	Lürssen	Nov 1980
Rodqm	P4503	Lürssen	Jul 1981
Shaheen	P4504	Lürssen	Jul 1981
Sagar	P4505	Lürssen	Sep 1981
Tarif	P4506	Lürssen	Sep 1981

Notes

Ordered in 1979, these FAC(M/G)s were the world's first operational craft with the longer-range MM.40 version of the Aérospatiale Exocet, and it is believed that the UAE may order more of the type in the near future. Some 350 rounds are carried for the 76mm (3in) OTO Melara L/62 dual-purpose gun in an OTO Melara Compact single mounting.

"Lürssen FPB/PB-57" class
(Germany/Spain)

Type: Fast attack craft (gun [missile])

Displacement: 275 tons standard and 393 tons full load

Dimensions: Length 190ft 7in (58.1m); beam 25ft 0in (7.62m); draught 9ft 3in (2.8m)

Gun armament: One 76mm (3in) OTO Melara L/62 dual-purpose gun in an OTO Melara Compact single mounting, one 40mm Bofors L/70 anti-aircraft gun in a Breda single mounting, and two 20mm Oerlikon-Bührle KAA L/85 anti-aircraft guns in Oerlikon-Bührle GAM-B01 single mountings

Missile armament: Generally none, but provision is made for two twin container-launchers for four McDonnell Douglas RGM-84 Harpoon anti-ship missiles

Torpedo armament: None

Anti-submarine armament: Generally none, but provision is made for two triple 12.75in (324mm) Mk 32 mountings for Mk 46 torpedoes, and two depth-charge racks

Electronics: One surface-search and tracking radar used in conjunction with one Hollandse Signaalapparaten WM-22/41 fire-control system, one Raytheon TM 1620/6X navigation radar, one HSM Mk 22 optical director, provision for one ELAC active search and attack hull sonar, and one ESM system with warning element

Propulsion: Diesel arrangement with two Bazan (MTU) MA15 TB91 diesel engines delivering a total of 8,045hp (6,000kW) to two shafts

Performance: Maximum speed 31kt; range 7,490 miles (12,050km) at 17kt or 3,105 miles (5,000km) at 28kt

Complement: 4+26 plus provision for 2 spare men

The Damisa, second of the Nigerian navy's three "Lürssen FPB-57" class of FAC(M/G)s, reveals the disposition of its gun and missile armaments while running high-speed trials before delivery.

Germany ("Type 143A" or "Gepard" class)

Name	No.	Builder	Commissioned
Gepard	P6121	AEG/Lürssen	Dec 1982
Puma	P6122	AEG/Lürssen	Feb 1983
Hermelin	P6123	AEG/Kröger	May 1983
Nerz	P6124	AEG/Lürssen	Jul 1983
Zobel	P6125	AEG/Telefunken	Sep 1983
Frettchen	P6126	AEG/Telefunken	Dec 1983
Dachs	P6127	AEG/Telefunken	Mar 1984
Ozelot	P6128	AEG/Lürssen	May 1984
Wiesel	P6129	AEG/Kröger	Jul 1984
Hyäne	P6130	AEG/Kröger	Nov 1984

Notes

Ordered in mid-1978 as replacements for the "Zobel" class FAC(T)s, these German FAC(M/G)s are built to a modified "Lürssen FPB-57" class design, with standard and full-load displacements of 295 and 391 tons respectively on dimensions that include a length of 189ft 4in (57.7m), beam of 24ft 11in (7.6m) and draught of 8ft 3in (2.5m). The missile armament comprises two twin container-launchers for four

Aérospatiale MM.38 Exocet anti-ship missiles, and the other weapons consist of one 76mm (3in) OTO Melara L/62 dual-purpose gun in an OTO Melara Compact single mounting and (being retrofitted) one EX-31 launcher for 24 General Dynamics RIM-116 RAM surface-to-air missiles; the type can also be equipped for minelaying. The electronics fit includes one surface-search and tracking radar used in conjunction with one Hollandse Signaalapparaten WM-27 fire-control system, one SMA 3RM 20 navigation radar, one AEG AGIS action information system, one ESM system with AEG FL1800 warning element, and one Buck-Wegmann Hot Dog/Silver Dog chaff/flare launcher. The propulsion arrangement of four MTU 16V 956 SB80 diesel engines delivers a total of 17,970hp (13,400kW) to four shafts for a maximum speed of 40kt and a range of 3,000 miles (4,825km) at 16kt. The complement is 4+30.

Germany ("Type 143B" or "Albatros" class)

Name	No.	Builder	Commissioned
Albatros	P6111	Lürssen	Nov 1976
Falke	P6112	Lürssen	Apr 1976
Geier	P6113	Lürssen	Jun 1976
Bussard	P6114	Lürssen	Aug 1976
Sperber	P6115	Kröger	Sep 1976
Greif	P6116	Lürssen	Nov 1976
Kondor	P6117	Kröger	Dec 1976
Seeadler	P6118	Lürssen	Mar 1977
Habicht	P6119	Kröger	Dec 1977
Kormoran	P6120	Lürssen	Jul 1977

Notes

Ordered in 1972 as replacements for the "Jaguar" class FAC(T)s, these German FAC(M/G/T)s were originally of the "Type 143" class with an armament of two twin container-launchers for four Aérospatiale MM.38 Exocet anti-ship missiles, two 76mm (3in) OTO Melara L/62 dual-purpose guns in two OTO Melara Compact single mountings, and two single 21in (533mm) mountings for two wire-guided heavyweight anti-ship torpedoes. The after 76mm (3in) mounting has been removed for installation on "Type 143A" class craft, and one EX-31 launcher for 24 RIM-116 RAM surface-to-air missiles is being installed in what has now become the "Type 143B" class. The displacement, dimensions and electronics are the same as those for the 'Type 143A' class, but the propulsion arrangement comprises four MTU 16V 956 TB91 diesel engines delivering a total of 21,460hp (16,000kW) to four shafts for a maximum speed of 40kt and a range of 1,490 miles (2,400km) at 30kt. The complement is 4+36.

Ghana (Lürssen FPB/PB-57 class)			
Name	*No.*	*Builder*	*Commissioned*
Achimota	P28	Lürssen	Dec 1979
Yogaga	P29	Lürssen	May 1980

Notes
Ordered in 1977, these Ghanaian FAC(G)s are of the original "Lürssen PB-57" type. The craft each have standard and full-load displacements of 380 and 410 tons respectively on dimensions that include a length of 190ft 7in (58.1m), beam of 25ft 0in (7.62m) and draught of 9ft 10in (3.0m). The armament comprises one 76mm (3in) OTO Melara L/62

Seen here while undertaking its sea trials before the completion of the armament fit, the Achimota of the Ghanaian navy reveals the considerable size of the area abaft the super-structure block of the "Lürssen PB-57" class available for additional guns and/or missile container-launchers.

Seen during builder's trials, this is one of the Kuwaiti navy's two "Lürssen FPB-57" class FAC(M/G)s, one of which was sunk in the 1991 Gulf War.

conjunction with one Bofors Electronics 9LV 228 fire-control system, one CSEE Lynx optical director, one Marconi Matilda ESM system with Marconi Cutlass-E warning and Marconi Cygnus jamming elements, and one CSEE Dagaie chaff/flare launcher. The propulsion arrangement comprises four MTU 16V 956 TB91 diesel engines delivering a total of 17,970hp (13,400kW) to four shafts for a maximum speed of 36kt and a range of 4,150 miles (6,675km) at 15kt declining to 1,725 miles (2,780km) at 31.2kt. The complement is 5+35, plus provision for two VIPs and 18 trainees (4 officers and 14 ratings). A sister vessel, the *Sabhan*, delivered by Lürssen in March 1983, was lost after the Iraqi invasion of Kuwait in 1990.

Morocco ("Lazaga [Modified]" class)

Name	No.	Builder	Commissioned
El Khattabi	304	Bazan	Jul 1981
Commandant Azouggargh	305	Bazan	Aug 1982
Commandant Boutouba	306	Bazan	Nov 1981
Commandant El Harty	307	Bazan	Feb 1982

Notes

Ordered in June 1977, these Moroccan FAC(M/G)s were derived from the Spanish vessels, and have a full-load displacement of 425 tons on dimensions that include a length of 190ft 7in (58.1m), beam of 25ft 0in (7.62m) and draught of 8ft 10in (2.7m). The missile armament comprises two twin container-launchers for four Aérospatiale MM.38 Exocet anti-ship missiles, and the other weapons consist of one 76mm (3in) OTO Melara L/62 dual-purpose gun in an OTO Melara Compact single mounting (300 rounds), one 40mm Bofors L/70 anti-aircraft gun in a single Breda mounting (1,472 rounds), and two 20mm Oerlikon-Bührle KAA L/90 anti-aircraft guns in Oerlikon-Bührle GAM-B01 single mountings (1,300 rounds each); there is no torpedo or anti-submarine armament. The electronics fit includes one Hollandse Signaalapparaten ZW-06 surface-search radar, one Decca TM1229C navigation radar, one tracking radar used in conjunction with one Hollandse Signaalapparaten WM-25 fire-control system, and one CSEE Panda optical director. The propulsion arrangement comprises two Bazan (MTU) 16V 956 TB91 diesel engines delivering a total of 8,050hp (6,000kW) to two shafts for a maximum speed of 30kt and a range of 3,420 miles (5,500km) at 15kt. The complement is 41.

Nigeria (Lürssen FPB/PB-57 class)

Name	No.	Builder	Commissioned
Ekpe	P178	Lürssen	Aug 1981
Damisa	P179	Lürssen	Apr 1981
Agu	P180	Lürssen	Apr 1981

Notes

Ordered in November 1977, these Nigerian FAC(M/G)s are based on the standard "Lürssen FPB-57" class hull with a full-load displacement of 444 tons on dimensions that include a length of 190ft 7in (58.1m), beam of 25ft 0in (7.62m) and draught of 10ft 3in (3.1m). The missile armament comprises four single container-launchers for four OTO Melara/Matra Otomat Mk 1 anti-ship missiles, and the other weapons consist of one 76mm (3in) OTO Melara L/62 dual-purpose gun in an OTO Melara Compact single mounting (250 rounds), two 40mm Bofors L/70 anti-aircraft guns in a Breda Compact twin mounting, and four 30mm

Oerlikon-Bührle KCB L/85 anti-aircraft guns in two EMERLEC-30 twin mountings. It was planned that two single 21in (533mm) mountings should be shipped for AEG Seal wire-guided heavyweight anti-ship torpedoes, but these were never installed. The electronics fit includes one Thomson-CSF Triton air/surface-search radar, one tracking radar used in conjunction with one Hollandse Signaalapparaten WM-28/41 fire-control system, and one ESM system with Decca RDL-2ABC warning element. The propulsion arrangement comprises four MTU 16V 956 TB92 diesel engines delivering a total of 20,120hp (15,000kW) to four shafts for a maximum speed of 42kt and a range of 2,300 miles (3,700km) at 16kt declining to 775 miles (1,250km) at 36kt. The complement is 7+45 plus provision for two spare officers.

The Dogan is the lead unit of the Turkish navy's eight-strong force of "Lürssen FPB-57" class FAC(M/G)s with powerful missile and gun armament.

Spain ("Lazaga" class)

Name	No.	Builder	Commissioned
Lazaga	P01	Lürssen	Jul 1975
Alsedo	P02	Bazan	Feb 1977
Cadarso	P03	Bazan	Jul 1976
Villamil	P04	Bazan	Apr 1977
Bonifaz	P05	Bazan	Jul 1977
Recalde	P06	Bazan	Dec 1977

Notes

Ordered in 1972, and with low performance as a result of a two-engine/two-shaft propulsion arrangement, these "Lürssen PB-57" class craft are used mainly for patrol and training, with provision for conversion into anti-ship and anti-submarine FAC(M)s with additional sensors and weapons.

Turkey ("Dogan" class)

Name	No.	Builder	Commissioned
Dogan	P340	Lürssen	Jun 1977
Marti	P341	Taskizak NY	Jul 1978
Tayfun	P342	Taskizak NY	Jul 1979
Volkan	P343	Taskizak NY	Jul 1980
Ruzgar	P344	Taskizak NY	Dec 1984
Poyraz	P345	Taskizak NY	Feb 1986
Gurbet	P346	Taskizak NY	Jul 1988
Firtina	P347	Taskizak NY	Oct 1988

Notes

These Turkish FAC(M/G)s, of which the first was ordered in August 1973, are to the standard "Lürssen FPB-57" class specification with standard and full-load displacements of 398 and 436 tons respectively on dimensions that include a length of 190ft 7in (58.1m), beam of 25ft 0in (7.62m) and draught of 9ft 3in (2.83m). The missile armament comprises two quadruple container-launchers for eight McDonnell Douglas RGM-84 Harpoon anti-ship missiles, and the other weapons consist of one 76mm (3in) OTO Melara L/62 dual-purpose gun in an OTO Melara Compact single mounting, and two 35mm Oerlikon-Bührle KDC L/90 anti-aircraft guns in an Oerlikon-Bührle GDM-A twin mounting. The electronics fit includes one Decca 1226 surface-search and navigation radar, one tracking radar used in conjunction with one Hollandse Signaalapparaten WM-28/41 fire-control system, one Hollandse Signaalapparaten optical director, one Marconi ESM system with Susie I warning element, and two multi-barrel chaff/flare launchers. The propulsion arrangement comprises four MTU 16V 956 TB91 diesel engines delivering a total of 17,970hp (13,400kW) to four shafts for a maximum speed of 38kt and a range of 1,490 miles (2,400km) at 26kt declining to 1,150 miles (1,850km) at 36kt. The complement is 5+33, plus provision for two spare men.

"Saar 4" or "Reshef" class
(Israel)

Type: Fast attack craft (missile and gun)

Displacement: 415 tons standard and 450 tons full load

Dimensions: Length 190ft 4in (58.0m); beam 25ft 7in (7.8m); draught 8ft 0in (2.4m)

Gun armament: One 76mm (3in) OTO Melara L/62 dual-purpose gun in an OTO Melara Compact single mounting (not in *Tarshish*), one 20mm General Electric Mk 26 six-barrel rotary cannon in a General Dynamics Phalanx Mk 15 CIWS mounting, two 20mm Hispano-Suiza HS-804 L/75 anti-aircraft guns in Oerlikon-Bührle A41A single mountings, and two 0.5in (12.7mm) Browning machine-guns in single mountings

Missile armament: One twin or quadruple Mk 141 container-launcher for two or four McDonnell Douglas RGM-84 Harpoon anti-ship missiles, or four or six single container-launchers for four or six IAI Gabriel II or III anti-ship missiles (or a mix of the two missile types)

Torpedo armament: None

Anti-submarine armament: None

Aircraft: Provision for one Mata Hellstar remotely piloted light helicopter on a platform aft (on *Tarshish* only)

Electronics: One Thomson-CSF TH-D 1040 Neptune air/surface-search radar, one Selenia Orion RTN 10X tracking radar used in conjunction with one Selenia Argo NA10 fire-control system, one IAI Reshet data-link system, one EDO 780 active/passive variable-depth sonar (not in *Yaffo*), one Elta ESM system with Elta MN-53 warning and jamming elements, nine or 11 chaff launchers (one 45-tube, four or six 24-tube and four 1-tube)

Propulsion: Diesel arrangement with four MTU 16V 956 TB91 diesel engines delivering a total of 13,950hp (10,400kW) to four shafts

Performance: Maximum speed 32kt; range 4,600 miles (7,400km) at 17.5kt or 1,910 miles (3,075km) at 30kt

Complement: 45

Chile			
Name	*No.*	*Builder*	*Commissioned*
Casma	30	Haifa Shipyard	May 1974
Chipana	31	Haifa Shipyard	Oct 1973

Notes

These Chilean FAC(M/G)s are similar to the original Israeli norm, but have a missile armament of four single container-launchers for four IAI Gabriel anti-ship missiles, while the other weapons consist of two 76mm (3in) OTO Melara L/62 dual-purpose guns in OTO Melara Compact single mountings and two 20mm Hispano-Suiza HS-804 L/75 anti-aircraft guns in Oerlikon-Bührle A41A single mountings, and a less-sophisticated sensor fit based on one Thomson-CSF Neptune surface-search and navigation radar used in conjunction with one Elta EL/M-2221 fire-control system; each vessel also possesses four Israeli chaff launchers. The craft (ex-*Romat* and ex-*Keshet*) were transferred to Chile in 1979 and 1981 respectively. Chile planned to build more of the type under licence, but the normalisation of relations with Argentina following the Vatican's settlement of the Beagle Canal dispute may have caused the cancellation of the plan, especially as the country bought two "Saar 3" class FACs from Israel in 1989.

Israel			
Name	*No.*	*Builder*	*Commissioned*
Reshef		Haifa Shipyard	Apr 1973
Kidon		Haifa Shipyard	Sep 1974
Tarshish		Haifa Shipyard	Mar 1975
Yaffo		Haifa Shipyard	Apr 1975
Nitzhon		Haifa Shipyard	Sep 1978
Atsmout		Haifa Shipyard	Feb 1979
Moledet		Haifa Shipyard	May 1979
Komemiut		Haifa Shipyard	Aug 1980

Notes

These are exceptional FAC(M/G)s built to a basic design from Lürssen but adapted to Israeli requirements to produce long-range craft with very good sea-keeping qualities and devastating missile armament. The extension of this armament has led to the modification of the original gun armament, which is reflected in the fit carried by the Chilean craft. Israel plans to replace the CIWS mounting with a vertical-launch system for Barak I surface-to-air missiles.

South Africa ("Minister" class)			
Name	No.	Builder	Commissioned
Jan Smuts	P1561	Haifa Shipyard	Sep 1977
P.W.Botha	P1562	Haifa Shipyard	Dec 1977
Frederic Cresswell	P1563	Haifa Shipyard	May 1978
Jim Fouche	P1564	Sandock Austral	Dec 1978
Frans Erasmus	P1565	Sandock Austral	Jul 1979
Oswald Pirow	P1566	Sandock Austral	Mar 1980
Hendrik Mentz	P1567	Sandock Austral	Sep 1982
Kobie Coetzee	P1568	Sandock Austral	Mar 1983
Magnus Malan	P1569	Sandock Austral	Jul 1986

Notes

Ordered in late 1974, these South African FAC(M/G)s are a variation on the Israeli norm, with a full-load displacement of 430 tons on dimensions that include a length of 204ft 0in (62.2m), beam of 25ft 7in (7.8m) and draught of 8ft 0in (2.4m). The missile armament comprises six single container-launchers for six Skorpioen (IAI Gabriel II) anti-ship missiles, and the other weapons consist of two 76mm (3in) OTO Melara L/62 dual-purpose guns in OTO Melara Compact single mountings, two 20mm Hispano-Suiza HS-804 L/75 anti-aircraft guns in Oerlikon-Bührle A41A single mountings and two 0.5in (12.7mm) Browning machine-guns in single mountings. The electronics fit, propulsion and performance are similar to those of the Israeli craft, and the complement is 7+40. It is reported that another three units are to be built to an improved standard.

"Willemoes" class
(Denmark)

Type: Fast attack craft (missile, gun and torpedo)

Displacement: 260 tons full load

Dimensions: Length 150ft 11in (46.0m); beam 24ft 0in (7.4m); draught 8ft 3in (2.5m)

Gun armament: One 76mm (3in) OTO Melara L/62 dual-purpose gun in an OTO Melara Compact single mounting

Missile armament: Two single or twin Mk 141 container-launchers for two or four McDonnell Douglas RGM-84 Harpoon anti-ship missiles

Torpedo armament: Two or four single 21in (533mm) mountings for two or four FFV Tp 61 wire-guided/passive acoustic-homing heavyweight anti-ship torpedoes

Anti-submarine armament: None

Electronics: One Bofors Electronics 9GR 208 air/surface-search radar, one Terma 20T 48 Super navigation radar, one Bofors Electronics 9LV 200 tracking radar used in conjunction with one Bofors Electronics 9LV 228 fire-control system, one EPLO (being replaced by Terma) action information system, and one ESM system with Racal Cutlass warning element

Propulsion: CODOG arrangement with three Rolls-Royce (Bristol) Proteus 52M/544 gas turbines delivering a total of 12,750hp (9,510kW) and two General Motors 8V-71 diesel engines delivering a total of 1,600hp (1,195kW) to three shafts

Performance: Maximum speed 38kt on gas turbines or 12kt on diesel engines

Complement: 5+20

The Bille was completed as the first of the Danish navy's 10-strong "Willemoes" class of highly capable FAC(M/G/T)s with a 3in (76mm) OTO Melara gun complemented by Harpoon anti-ship missiles and wire-guided heavyweight torpedoes whose numbers can be altered in relation to each other. The vessel is seen here with four 21in (533mm) mountings for torpedoes: the after pair of tubes can be replaced by two single or twin container-launchers for Harpoon missiles.

Denmark

Name	No.	Builder	Commissioned
Bille	P540	Frederikshavn Vaerft	Oct 1976
Bredal	P541	Frederikshavn Vaerft	Jan 1977
Hammer	P542	Frederikshavn Vaerft	Apr 1977
Huitfeld	P543	Frederikshavn Vaerft	Jun 1977
Krieger	P544	Frederikshavn Vaerft	Sep 1977
Norby	P545	Frederikshavn Vaerft	Nov 1977
Rodsteen	P546	Frederikshavn Vaerft	Feb 1978
Sehested	P547	Frederikshavn Vaerft	May 1978
Suenson	P548	Frederikshavn Vaerft	Aug 1978
Willemoes	P549	Frederikshavn Vaerft	Jun 1976

Notes

On the south-western side of the Baltic Sea lies Denmark, a member of the NATO alliance. Although small, Denmark is of crucial importance to the Western alliance as it dominates the Kattegat, the eastern half of the exit from the Baltic Sea into the North Sea. As such, the Danish navy has long been ideally placed to prevent any movement of the Soviet (now Russian) Baltic Fleet out of its eponymous sea. The Danish navy also possesses a wider-ranging role, but for operations in the shallow western part of the Baltic Sea it relies on a force of small submarines and fast combat craft. In the late 1950s, the Danish navy ordered a new class of FAC(T)s based on the German *Schnellboote* concept of World War II. These four craft were the units of the "Falken" class, and were commissioned in the early 1960s. With a displacement of 119 tons and a length of 117ft 9in (35.9m), each of these craft was powered by three Mercedes-Benz diesel engines delivering a total of 9,060hp (6,750kW) and carried as primary armament four 21in (533mm) torpedoes. These torpedoes were located in two tubes on each side of the deck, and the rest of the armament comprised one 40mm Bofors gun over the stern and one 20mm cannon in a well on the forecastle.

This four-craft class was essentially a stopgap, and considerably greater capability was provided by the six FAC(T)s of the "Síliven" class, a derivative of the British "Brave" class design. The first two units were built by Vosper at Portsmouth, and the other four by the Royal Dockyard in Copenhagen. The armament is an improved version of that carried by the "Falken" class, with four torpedo tubes and two 40mm Bofors guns. The forward gun was located on the forecastle in an open mounting, while the after gun was located over the stern and could be enclosed in a weatherproof turret, although this demanded that the two after torpedo tubes be unshipped. The real advantage of the "Søløven" class over the "Falken" class lay in its CODOG propulsion arrangement, however, with two diesel engines powering the wing propellers for a quiet cruising speed of 10kt but shut down in favour of three Rolls-Royce (Bristol) Proteus gas turbines delivering a total of 12,750hp (9,505kW) to all three shafts for the highly impressive maximum speed of 54kt. Libya ordered three slightly different craft as the "Susa" class that is still in service with the same propulsion arrangement and similar performance on a slightly modified hull, with the decidedly indifferent missile armament of eight container-launchers for the Aérospatiale (Nord) SS.12M short-range missile, a naval version of the AS.12 wire-guided missile designed for helicopter launch against targets such as bunkers and other fixed defences.

By the early 1970s, the Danish navy had appreciated that the days of the small FAC(T) were numbered, and that continued viability of its fast combat craft force depended on the adoption of a more advanced type. As the core of its new German-designed "Willemoes" class, the service selected the hull of the Swedish "Spica II" class with a CODOG propulsion arrangement for a long-range cruising speed of 12kt and a combat speed of 38kt. The class was commissioned between 1976 and 1978, the early units in FAC(G/T) form with one 76mm (3in) OTO Melara L/62 dual-purpose gun in an OTO Melara Compact mounting on the forecastle and four 21in (533mm) tubes for Swedish wire-guided heavyweight anti-ship torpedoes. The aim was to create an FAC(M/G/T) type, however, with the McDonnell Douglas RGM-84 Harpoon anti-ship missile that became available only in the late 1970s. Although it is possible to replace the complete torpedo armament with missiles, the standard fit includes both torpedoes and missiles, with the two after torpedo tubes replaced by two single or twin container-launchers for this important missile.

The same missile type can be installed on Denmark's latest type of FAC, the Standard Flex 300 design being produced as the "Flyvevisken" class, of which 16 units have been projected. This was conceived as a very economical type with a straightforward hull and a CODAG propulsion arrangement, in which the two wing shafts are powered by diesel engines and the central shaft is powered by either one electric motor or one gas turbine. Use of just the two wing shafts produces an economical cruising speed of 20kt, while the central shaft can be used on its own in the electrically powered mode for a virtually silent creeping speed of 6kt or, in concert with the other two shafts in gas-turbine powered mode, for the respectable maximum speed of 30kt. The type is made particularly cost-effective by its use of the modern concept of modular or "plug-in" weapons and electronics. Thus the craft are being delivered in FAC(G) form with one 76mm (3in) OTO Melara L/62 dual-purpose gun in an OTO Melara Super Rapid mounting, and a basic electronic suite that includes a comparatively simple surface-search radar with the advanced Bofors Electronics 9LV 200 Mk 3 Sea Viking fire-control system that includes optronic and thermal sights as well as a laser rangefinder. In this form the type replaces the nine "Daphne" class seaward defence vessels, but can be retrofitted with specialised electronics and weapons to replace the eight "Sund" class coastal minesweepers and/or the six "Søløven" class FAC(T)s. In its maximum-capability form, the "Flyvevisken" class design is that of an FAC(M/G/T) with the 76mm gun complemented by four anti-ship missiles, one surface-to-air missile system and two 21in (533mm) wire-guided heavyweight torpedoes.